DATE DUE

DEMCO 38-297

BASEBALL LEGENDS

Hank Aaron
Grover Cleveland Alexander
Ernie Banks
Johnny Bench
Yogi Berra
Roy Campanella
Roberto Clemente
Ty Cobb
Dizzy Dean
Joe DiMaggio
Bob Feller
Jimmie Foxx
Lou Gehrig
Bob Gibson
Rogers Hornsby
Walter Johnson
Sandy Koufax
Mickey Mantle
Christy Mathewson
Willie Mays
Stan Musial
Satchel Paige
Brooks Robinson
Frank Robinson
Jackie Robinson
Babe Ruth
Duke Snider
Warren Spahn
Willie Stargell
Honus Wagner
Ted Williams
Carl Yastrzemski
Cy Young

CHELSEA HOUSE PUBLISHERS

BASEBALL LEGENDS

FRANK ROBINSON

Norman L. Macht

Introduction by
Jim Murray

Senior Consultant
Earl Weaver

CHELSEA HOUSE PUBLISHERS
New York • Philadelphia

Produced by James Charlton Associates
New York, New York.

Designed by Hudson Studio
Ossining, New York.

Typesetting by LinoGraphics
New York, New York.

Picture research by Carolann Hawkins
Cover illustration by Dan O'Leary

First Printing

1 3 5 7 9 8 6 4 2

Library of Congress Cataloging-in-Publication Data

Macht, Norman L. (Norman Lee), 1929-
    Frank Robinson / Norman Macht ; introduction by Jim Murray ;
  senior consultant, Earl Weaver.
      p. cm.—(Baseball legends)
    Includes bibliographical references (p.) and index.
    Summary: Follows the life and career of baseball star Frank
  Robinson, who became the first black manager in the major leagues.
    ISBN 0-7910-1221-2.—ISBN 0-7910-1187-9 (pbk.)
    1. Robinson, Frank, 1935- —Juvenile literature. 2. Baseball
  players—United States—Biography—Juvenile literature.
    3. Baseball—United States—Managers—Biography—Juvenile
  literature. [1. Robinson, Frank, 1935- . 2. Baseball players.
    3. Baseball—Managers. 4. Afro-Americans—Biography.] I. Title.
  II. Series.
  GV865.R59M33 1991
    92—dc20   90-38510
    [796.357'092]   CIP
    [B]   AC

CONTENTS

WHAT MAKES A STAR

Jim Murray

No one has ever been able to explain to me the mysterious alchemy that makes one man a .350 hitter and another player, more or less identical in physical makeup, hard put to hit .200. You look at an Al Kaline, who played with the Detroit Tigers from 1953 to 1974. He was pale, stringy, almost poetic-looking. He always seemed to be struggling against a bad case of mononucleosis. But with a bat in his hands, he was King Kong. During his career, he hit 399 home runs, rapped out 3,007 hits, and compiled a .297 batting average.

Form isn't the reason. The first time anybody saw Roberto Clemente step into the batter's box for the Pittsburgh Pirates, the best guess was that Clemente would be back in Double A ball in a week. He had one foot in the bucket and held his bat at an awkward angle—he looked as though he couldn't hit an outside pitch. A lot of other ballplayers may have had a better-looking stance. Yet they never led the National League in hitting in four different years, the way Clemente did.

Not every ballplayer is born with the ability to hit a curveball. Nor is exceptional hand-eye coordination the key to heavy hitting. Big-league locker rooms are filled with players who have all the attributes, save one: discipline. Every baseball man can tell you a story about a pitcher who throws a ball faster than anyone has ever seen but who has no control on or *off* the field.

The Hall of Fame is full of people who transformed themselves into great ballplayers by working at the sport, by studying the game, and making sacrifices. They're overachievers—and winners. If you want to find them, just watch the World Series. Or simply read about New York Yankee great Lou Gehrig; Ted Williams, "the Splendid Splinter" of the Boston Red Sox; or the Dodgers' strikeout king Sandy Koufax.

A pitcher *should* be able to win a lot of ballgames with a 98-miles-per-hour fastball. But what about the pitcher who wins 20 games a year with a fastball so slow that you can catch it with your teeth? Bob Feller of the Cleveland Indians got into the Hall of Fame with a blazing fastball that glowed in the dark. National League star Grover Cleveland Alexander got there with a pitch that took considerably longer to reach the plate; but when it did arrive, the pitch was exactly where Alexander wanted it to be—and the last place the batter expected it to be.

There are probably more players with exceptional ability who didn't make it to the major leagues than there are who did. A number of great hitters, bored with fielding practice, had to be dropped from their team because their home-run production didn't make up for their lapses in the field. And then there are players like Brooks Robinson of the Baltimore Orioles, who made himself into a human vacuum cleaner at third base because he knew that working hard to become an expert fielder would win him a job in the big leagues.

A star is not something that flashes through the sky. That's a comet. Or a meteor. A star is something you can steer ships by. It stays in place and gives off a steady glow; it is fixed, permanent. A star works at being a star.

And that's how you tell a star in baseball. He shows up night after night and takes pride in how brightly he shines. He's Willie Mays running so hard his hat keeps falling off; Ty Cobb sliding to stretch a single into a double; Lou Gehrig, after being fooled in his first two at-bats, belting the next pitch off the light tower because he's taken the time to study the pitcher. Stars never take themselves for granted. That's why they're stars.

A LEADER IS BORN

On the night of February 8, 1961, Frank Robinson, superstar outfielder for the Cincinnati Reds, sat in a dingy jail cell. He was charged with carrying a concealed weapon, a palm-sized pistol that he had pulled from his pocket when the anger, frustration, and resentment inside him had boiled over.

A free-spending bachelor of 25 who earned $30,000 a year, Robinson enjoyed carrying a big bankroll wherever he went. He told the police that he needed the gun for protection. But even as he said it, he realized he was really carrying it just to prove he was a man.

Robinson and two friends, both of whom were black, had stopped at an all-night diner that evening. Three white youths were inside. Some fighting words were exchanged between the

In the seventh inning of game 4 of the 1961 World Series, Frank Robinson and Reds second baseman Elio Chacon chase a pop fly hit by Yogi Berra. The two collided on the play and the Yankees scored the tieing run. The Yankees went on to win the game, 4-1, and the Series by the same margin.

youths and Robinson's group and a brawl started. While the cook summoned two policemen who were in a patrol car outside, the white men slipped out of the diner. That would have been the end of it if the policeman had not called Robinson and his buddies "you boys." Calling black men "boys" was taken as a put-down, an inference of inferiority, and one of them reacted angrily. The police arrested Robinson's friend for disturbing the peace and took him to the station.

After Robinson put up $100 in bail to have his friend released from jail, all three of them returned defiantly to the restaurant. The cook promptly stuck out his head from the kitchen and saw the three. Waving a knife, he drew a finger across his throat to indicate that they would get theirs. That gesture infuriated the hot-tempered Robinson, who jumped up and pulled the gun from his jacket pocket.

"If you think you're a big man, come on," he yelled.

The cook hollered for the two policemen, who were outside the diner. When they came in, Robinson stuck the gun back in his pocket, but they frisked him and found it. He was arrested for carrying a concealed weapon.

Frank Robinson spent the long night on a bunk in the cell, choking back tears. Ever since he was the age of six, he had wanted only one thing: to be a big-league ballplayer. He had fought off loneliness, injuries, and racial prejudice in the minor leagues to get there, earning Rookie of the Year honors in 1956, his first year with the Reds. Although Robinson was considered the best player on the team, he was far from the most popular. Robinson knew that some of the other players thought he was only out for himself. It did not seem

Frank Robinson awaits his sentence in March 1961 for carrying a concealed weapon. He pleaded guilty and was fined $250.

to bother him if the team lost, as long as he got his hits. But now, as he sat alone in the heavy darkness, he began to understand how much more he could do for the team, and what they could do for him. He thought of other players who had less ability than he, yet who seemed to be putting out so much more. And he knew he could do better.

When a bondsman secured his release in the morning, Robinson was determined to prove himself in the only way that counted: on the playing field. He could only hope he would be given the chance.

As it turned out, Reds manager Fred Hutchinson mentioned the incident just once. "It was a stupid thing to do," he said.

"Yes," Robinson agreed, "but sometimes a man learns from his stupidities."

Three weeks later Robinson returned to Cincinnati from spring training to plead guilty as charged and was fined $250. He paid the money and threw away the gun.

"It turned out to be the best thing that ever

happened to me," he later acknowledged. "It made me grow up."

It turned out to be the *worst* thing that ever happened to the Reds' rivals, however. Robinson shrugged off the inevitable riding from players and fans about the gun incident and simply tore up the National League. He became a leader by example and attitude. Even when he was hurting from arm and knee injuries, he stayed in the lineup and played like a man possessed. He hit game-winning home runs, made incredible catches, and pulled daring baserunning maneuvers. On May 9, 1963, he had one of the biggest days of his life, driving in seven runs with two homers and a double after being hit by a pitch. During one stretch he reached base 17 times in 19 at-bats, including three doubles in one game. More important, he stirred his team-mates to greater achievements by hollering from the sidelines—urging them on whenever they let up—and needling opposing pitchers.

Robinson came to understand what it meant to be a true leader. "If you can't swing the bat and run the bases and catch the balls and maybe a little more besides, nobody's going to follow you," he said. "You're just a little tin soldier waving a tin sword."

One day in early July Robinson saw his leadership role confirmed. Although the Reds were number one in the N.L., they had just dropped three out of four games to the Chicago Cubs and were heading into Milwaukee with their tails down. With their five-game lead over the Los Angeles Dodgers in jeopardy, Robinson called a team meeting. He stormed around the clubhouse, angrily chewing out the players for not playing heads-up ball, not being aggressive enough at bat or on the bases. Then he went out and batted .409 for the month, hitting 13 home runs and driving in 34 runs.

Despite Robinson's great effort, the Dodgers caught up with Cincinnati in August. Then the Reds took a one-game lead as the Cardinals came to Crosley Field, Cincinnati's ballpark, for an important series. In the first game the Reds were two runs behind when Robinson came up in the 8th inning with two men on and two out. Playing injured—he had twisted his knee sliding into a base—Robinson belted out a double that drove in the tying run. The Reds went on to win the ballgame, widening their lead to two games as the Dodgers lost. The next night, Robinson contributed the winning RBI in the 12th inning. Again the Dodgers lost, and now Cincinnati was up by three games. On September 26, a Robinson home run beat the Cubs to clinch the pennant.

Although the Reds lost the World Series to the New York Yankees, Robinson had plenty to celebrate. He had finished the season batting .323, with 37 home runs and 124 runs batted in. Three weeks after the World Series, he married Barbara Ann Cole, and soon after that, he was voted the National League's Most Valuable Player—as much for his leadership as his accomplishments on the field. Family man and team leader, Frank Robinson had come a long way from the jail cell.

2

FIRST STOP: OGDEN, UTAH

Born in Beaumont, Texas, on August 31, 1935, Frank Robinson was brought to California by his mother when his father left the family. By then, all but one of his six older brothers and three sisters were married or working, and they contributed to the family's support. Frank was a movie bug, a passion he never lost. When his mother suggested he earn his own movie money, he took a newspaper route, which he promptly turned over to a friend whenever there was a ballgame to be found.

The boys played ball indoors and out, in the streets, on empty lots, and in the schoolyard. From the start, Frank went all-out, tearing up his clothes by sliding on the asphalt or concrete surfaces. He played until it was dark and often missed supper; his mother got used to leaving a pot on the stove for him.

When Frank was growing up in Oakland, California, in the 1940s and 1950s, he lived in a neighborhood where there were white families and blacks, Mexicans and Orientals, and nobody made a big deal out of it. Frank was 11 years old when Jackie Robinson became the first black player to enter the major leagues. The historic significance of the event escaped Frank at the time, although he would later come to appreciate it. Frank played on some teams that were mostly black and others that were mostly white, but they were all the same to him. The only thing that mattered was that he was playing something—football and basketball in their seasons, but especially baseball.

Frank was a skinny kid and very shy. He kept his head down and walked with a sort of slouch that made him appear lackadaisical if not downright disinterested. It belied the intensity and aggressiveness with which he moved once the game began, and later caused people to accuse him of not hustling. He eventually grew to be 6'1", with a well-muscled upper body, but he always had thin legs that earned him the nickname "Pencils."

Frank was a student at Westlake Junior High when he met two men who would greatly influence his future: George Powles and Bobby Mattick. Powles was a coach at McClymonds High School, where he built many winning baseball and basketball teams. Powles devoted his life to helping young athletes develop their potential. He also coached several amateur teams. After watching Frank in a pickup game, he invited the 14-year-old to play on weekends for the Doll Drugstore team. All the other players were older. In his first game, Frank was sent in to pinch-hit, and he blasted a home run over the center fielder's head. He followed that with a triple his next time up, and from then on he was a regular starter.

The next year, Frank played third base on Powles's American Legion team, which won its second straight national championship in a tournament that took the boys to Arizona and Nebraska. Homesick and nervous in the strange cities, Frank did not play well.

The star of the team was J. W. Porter, a catcher who had received a $65,000 bonus to sign with the Chicago White Sox. A Chicago scout named Bobby Mattick was following the team to keep an eye on Porter. Mattick could not help noticing Robinson's quick, strong wrists, his power at the plate, and his drive and determination on the field. Less impressive, however, was Frank's play at third base. Mattick worked with the youngster and tutored him, but told him frankly that he would never make it to the big leagues as an infielder. Nevertheless, Frank preferred the action in the infield and continued playing third base. Batting .424 during his senior year in high school helped overshadow his deficiencies with the glove. He wound up making the all-city high school team three times.

When Frank was in high school, Coach Powles advised him to do pushups at home to strengthen his wrists and shoulders. Frank shook the house down doing his exercises. But when Mattick told him to give up football, lest an injury ruin his baseball chances, Frank ignored the advice. He scored several touchdowns as a halfback, but then got mashed in a game and had to be carried off the field on a stretcher. Only then did he decide to quit football.

Frank also played basketball at McClymonds, where one of his teammates was Bill Russell. Russell went on to become the star center and coach of the Boston Celtics, but it was Robinson who was the high scorer on the McClymonds team in 1952.

By then, Bobby Mattick had gone to work for the Cincinnati Reds. Nevertheless, he stayed in close touch with Frank and his family. Frank appreciated Mattick's interest, and after graduating from high school he signed with the Reds' Class C minor-league team for a bonus of $3,500 and a monthly salary of $400.

Before Frank left for the Reds' farm team in Ogden, Utah, Mattick gave him some good advice. Frank had a hitch in his swing—a slight hesitation as he prepared to bring the bat forward. Mattick suspected that some managers would try to eliminate it, and he told Frank to ignore them. The hitch, combined with his strong wrists, gave him enormous power.

Batting turned out to be the least of Robinson's

J.W. Porter, Frank's American Legion teammate, was the star on their national championship team. Porter made his major-league debut at the age of 19, but was never a star in the big leagues.

problems. The 17-year-old minor leaguer failed to run into any pitching he could not handle in the Pioneer League, but he ran smack into something else: racial prejudice. Few blacks lived in the state, and many of the whites treated blacks as though they were second-class citizens. The white players easily found rooms in private homes, but none were open to Frank or Chico Terry, a dark-skinned Hispanic who spoke almost no English. The two players shared a hotel room, unable to communicate with each other. Lonely and depressed, Frank sought escape in his favorite pastime, the movies. But even there his color made him unwelcome.

"We don't serve your kind," the ticket seller said.

It was not that way in the other towns in the league, but it was enough to cause the shy young man to turn even more inward. Over and over he kept telling himself, "This is the situation and you just have to make the best of it if you want to play major-league ball."

He made the best of it by batting .348 and hitting 17 home runs. Robinson, who finally realized that he was not a third baseman and switched to the outfield, could not have been happier when his fine performance earned him a promotion out of Ogden. But Utah would soon seem like an oasis of brotherly love compared to his next stop on the road to the majors.

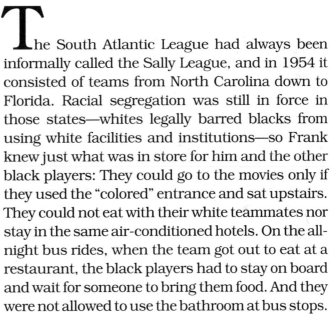

The South Atlantic League had always been informally called the Sally League, and in 1954 it consisted of teams from North Carolina down to Florida. Racial segregation was still in force in those states—whites legally barred blacks from using white facilities and institutions—so Frank knew just what was in store for him and the other black players: They could go to the movies only if they used the "colored" entrance and sat upstairs. They could not eat with their white teammates nor stay in the same air-conditioned hotels. On the all-night bus rides, when the team got out to eat at a restaurant, the black players had to stay on board and wait for someone to bring them food. And they were not allowed to use the bathroom at bus stops.

In the small ballparks, the fans sat so close to the players on the field it was impossible to tune out the racial taunts. Resentful and angry, Frank answered back the only way he could—by playing his hardest for the Columbia, South Carolina,

When Frank Robinson started his professional career in the 1950s, segregation was more apparent in the South than in the North. Many public facilities, such as city buses, still separated blacks and whites.

21

Cozy Crosley Field in Cincinnati was home to the Reds from 1884 until June 4, 1970, when the team moved into Riverfront Stadium. The first big league night game was played May 24, 1935, when President Franklin D. Roosevelt pushed a button in the White House to turn on the lights at Crosley Field.

Reds. He chanted to himself, "Have a good year and get out of here."

After one coach had thrown Robinson off his stride by trying to change his batting style, Columbia manager Ernie White told him to bat however he felt comfortable. Frank did just that and came through with a home run in his first game and three more the next night. At that rate, Robinson had reason to hope he would soon be promoted out of the Sally League. But while he did have an excellent year, batting .336, a perverse twist of fate prevented him from leaving the league. One day, he made a long, hard throw from the outfield and immediately experienced a sharp pain in his shoulder. It felt as if somebody had jabbed a pin in it. For the rest of the season, he felt pain every time he made a throw.

That winter he played in a league in Puerto Rico. On a deep throw, the pin jab became a knife stabbing his shoulder. Robinson went to one doctor after another, but the best they could tell him was to give it some rest.

In the spring of 1955, Frank's shoulder felt

much better when he reported to the Reds. He so impressed Cincinnati manager Birdie Tebbetts with his hitting that Tebbetts decided to make the 19-year-old rookie his starting left fielder. But the pain came back. His shoulder swelled, and he could not even throw a ball across a room. Reluctantly, the Reds sent him back to Columbia and the Sally League.

Robinson became more angry and frustrated with each passing day. When he played, his sore shoulder kept him from doing his best. All this spurred the fans to blast him with vicious racial catcalls and slurs. Frank took it as long as he could. But then, after one particularly unpleasant game, he grabbed a bat and ran after three drunks in the grandstand. The manager stopped him before any damage was done and warned those fans not to show up at the park again. But Robinson knew there would be many others just like them.

Discouraged, Frank Robinson decided to quit baseball. When the team left on a road trip, he stayed behind and prepared to go home. The only other black player on the club, Marv Williams, an old minor-leaguer who had helped Frank with his hitting, stayed with him. The teammates talked all through the night, and by morning Frank realized that baseball was his whole life. He should not abandon his dream before he was even 20 years old. Williams and Robinson got a friend to drive them to Charlotte to rejoin the team.

With enough rest, Robinson's shoulder began to improve. Playing regularly and with more determination than ever, he batted .390 and blasted 10 home runs in the last six weeks to lead Columbia to a come-from-behind pennant victory. Free of pain, Frank Robinson had made his way out of the Sally League for good.

A FIERCE COMPETITOR

Birdie Tebbetts was the best kind of manager Frank Robinson could have had as a rookie in the major leagues. He gave the young outfielder confidence by starting him in left field on opening day of the 1956 season.

Tebbetts was an excellent teacher, and Robinson was eager to learn. When the youngster made a mistake, Tebbetts would take him aside and explain exactly what he had done wrong and how to correct it. He often sat Robinson beside him on the bench and explained why they played certain hitters the way they did, how to study the pitchers and plan one's next move. Robinson later credited Tebbetts with making him aware of the importance of being in the game—thinking, studying, watching—even when he was not actually playing.

Robinson got off to a fast start, hitting a double in his first big-league at-bat. "The batter ahead of me had just hit a home run off Vinegar Bend Mizell and that took the pressure off me," Robinson later recalled.

On April 28, Robinson hit the first of his 586 career home runs, off Paul Minner of the Cubs. He would hit 38 of them that first year, tying the

Rookie Frank Robinson is met at homeplate in 1956 by Ted Kluszewski. With "Big Klu," who cut off the sleeves of his uniform to give his big arms more room, batting behind him, Frank led the National League in runs scored with 122.

*Robinson hands out batting
tips at one of the Reds'
annual father-son games.*

National League home run record for rookies. He
also lead the league in runs scored (122) and batted
.290 with 83 RBIs. It came as no surprise when he
was named to the All-Star team and was the
unanimous choice for Rookie of the Year.

Frank Robinson could hardly have had a better
rookie season. Yet in some ways life in the big
leagues was not so different from the Sally League.
The black players all lived in a hotel for blacks only.
They did not mix, at home or on the road, with their
white teammates. The other blacks on the Reds
were older than Frank and showed little interest in
him. The veterans would usually go out to a
restaurant at night, and sometimes Robinson
tagged along. Although he enjoyed listening to
them talk baseball, he did not drink and did not
enjoy staying up late. As a result, he was often

alone, with nothing to do. On the day of a night game, he usually turned to his favorite fantasy land: the movies. The first one in when the theater opened in the morning, he sometimes watched as many as four movies in one day. This would be his primary way of relaxing for the next ten years.

There was nothing relaxed about Frank Robinson on the field, however. Determined to play to win any way he could within the rules, the young loner soon became one of the most feared players in the National League. Robinson never set out to hurt anyone, but he accepted that getting hurt was part of the game, and he expected other players to accept that, too. Even when he was out by a mile, he still did his best to bowl over the man with the ball. That just might cause the fielder to drop the ball, he reasoned, or to commit another kind of error. At the very least, it would make the fielder more cautious and wary the next time Robinson came to bat.

When his spikes opened a cut that took twenty stitches to close on the shin of Milwaukee's Johnny Logan, Robinson earned the reputation as a guy who cut down infielders. After he spiked the Dodgers' Don Zimmer at second base, Zimmer's teammate Duke Snider snarled "What are you trying to prove?" That puzzled Robinson because he had always thought of Snider as a hard baserunner who played all-out, too.

In the first game of a doubleheader, also against the Milwaukee Braves, Robinson slid into Ed Mathews at third base. Mathews brought his glove down hard on Robinson's nose, which caused it to bleed. The two players got into a shouting match, and then Mathews swung and hit Robinson in the eye. Robinson swung back. Mathews was quickly thrown out of the game, but by then Robinson could barely see out of his swollen right eye or breathe through his beat-up nose. Still, he managed to play in the second game, in which he was hit by a pitch, walked, singled, doubled, and hit a home run. He also robbed Mathews of a homer with a spectacular catch made by leaning over the left-field railing. Before the day ended, Mathews apologized. The incident was over. It was just part of the game—until the next time.

Robinson later explained his attitude: "I believe you should do everything to win short of hurting someone deliberately. If you're going into a second baseman, let him know you are going to knock him down, bump him, or do something every time, and he's going to be thinking about you every time." It was his way of gaining an edge on his opponent.

A tough, combative player is always resented by players on other teams, but when trades bring one-time bitter enemies together on the same team, the resentment quickly disappears. An aggressive player will not hesitate to knock down a former teammate when they change uniforms. There is nothing personal in it. It is the other uniform that is seen as the enemy, not the man inside it.

When Don Zimmer, who later became the Cubs' manager, was traded from the Dodgers to the Reds, he echoed most players' sentiments: "I hated Frank Robinson's guts when I played against him. But there's nothing dirty or mean about it, he just plays hard."

Robinson also proved willing to take the same kind of treatment he dished out. His arms became a mass of thick scars, where rival catchers and infielders came down with their sharp spikes. One cut on his left bicep took thirty stitches to close and kept him out of action for ten days. Once, when he was trying to steal home, the opposing catcher stepped on his forearm and the wound left a 5-inch ridge of hard scar tissue. Two fingers on his left hand are permanently crooked from being jammed into bases.

Infielders took the brunt of his baserunning, but as an outfielder and first baseman, Robinson was safe from their retaliation. It was up to the pitchers to get back at him—and they did. Knockdown pitches were expected; they were part of the game. The Dodgers and Phillies took aim at Robinson's head and body more than any other teams. But even when they were not trying, rival pitchers beaned him. They could hardly avoid it because Robinson crowded the plate so much that his head was actually over it. When pitchers tried to back him away by throwing inside, Robinson did not take it personally. All winning pitchers throw inside, he knew. But when they threw the ball behind him, he had no doubt they were trying to hit him, and angry fights often broke out. Robinson

Robinson suffered a severe concussion in an exhibition game against the Washington Senators in 1958. Reds trainer Wayne Anderson keeps a careful eye on the young star.

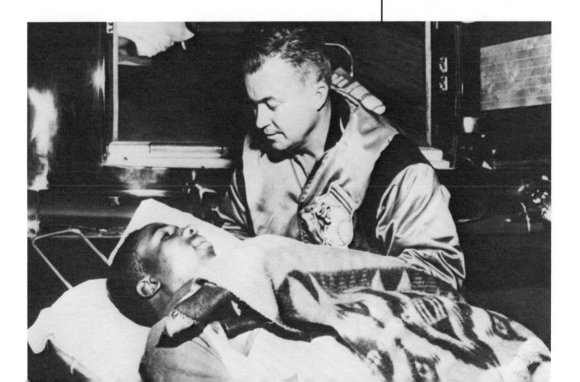

was hit by pitches 20 times in his first year and usually led the league in bruises.

Don Drysdale of the Dodgers once walked him intentionally by throwing at his head four times. But Robinson was not intimidated. Each time he got up from the dirt, he moved closer to the plate. Even players who hated Robinson respected him for his courage.

Pitchers soon learned that knocking Frank Robinson down only made him tougher at the plate. He did not charge the mound or wave a bat menacingly at them when they dusted him off. He had a better way of getting even—hitting the ball out of the park or driving in the game-winning run. At least one manager ordered his pitchers not to get Robinson riled up by throwing at him.

A pitch that was *not* meant to hit him almost finished Robinson's career. His second year with the Reds, 1957, was even more impressive than his debut: a .322 batting average, 29 home runs, and 75 RBIs. He seemed destined for superstardom. But in a pre-season exhibition game in 1958, Washington's Camilo Pascual threw a fastball that hit him behind the ear under his helmet. Robinson began the regular season with blurred vision and frequent headaches. He did not tell the manager about it and continued to play, but he became gun-shy at the plate. Anybody who has been knocked cold by a fastball, no matter how brave and fearless he may be, is going to be a little hesitant about stepping into another pitch—especially someone whose eyes do not focus properly. Robinson had no trouble hitting fastballs, but whenever a curve started in toward him, he would instinctively lean back—players call it "bailing out"—and when the ball broke over the plate he was unable to reach it. It was not long before the pitchers caught on and the word got around. They began throwing him nothing but the curve, and by midseason his average was down to .240.

Robinson did some hard thinking during the All-Star break and came back determined to lick his fear. In an exhibition game against a farm team, he vowed to stand in there no matter what the pitch and get the bat on the ball. He got two hits that day. The next day, in San Francisco, a pitcher threw Robinson the same kind of curve he had been leaning away from, but this time he stepped in and knocked it over the fence. He was so happy that he almost danced around the bases. His next at-bat was against Ruben Gomez, who had beaned him once before. This time Robinson held his ground and smacked the first pitch for a base hit.

Cured of his fear, Robinson hit 23 home runs in the last three months and lifted his 1958 batting average to a respectable .269.

•

5

UPS AND DOWNS

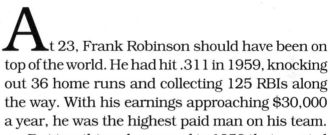

At 23, Frank Robinson should have been on top of the world. He had hit .311 in 1959, knocking out 36 home runs and collecting 125 RBIs along the way. With his earnings approaching $30,000 a year, he was the highest paid man on his team.

But two things happened in 1959 that worried Robinson. For starters, the Reds wanted him to play first base, a change he was reluctant to make. Then in the middle of the season, manager Birdie Tebbetts was fired and replaced by Fred Hutchinson. The new manager was known as "the Bear" because of his celebrated snarl and explosive temper.

An intense competitor who could not stand losing, Hutchinson was well liked and respected by players on every team. During the six years he managed the Reds, however, his own players knew to stay out of his way when Hutchinson's temper was up.

Dodgers pitcher Roger Craig knocks down Robinson in an August 14, 1960, game. Robinson's style at the plate often caused him to be hit by pitches. He set a rookie mark in 1956 when he was hit by pitches 20 times, and led the league in that category from 1960-66.

At first, Robinson did not know how to deal with the new manager. When Hutchinson was not blowing off steam, he was quiet, unlike the talkative Tebbetts, and seemed to be wearing a scowl all the time. Eventually, though, Robinson learned to appreciate Hutchinson and called him a "man's man" who stood up for his players.

A change in the Reds ownership made things worse for Robinson in 1960. He was again asked to play first base; he spent some frustrating time on the bench; and he got into a few fights on the field. As his batting average slipped below .260, his spirits sank, too. But he managed to turn things around once again, and he pulled his average up to .297 by the end of the year.

Still, the new Reds president, Bill DeWitt, wanted to cut Robinson's salary for 1961. According to DeWitt, Robinson was just not hustling enough. DeWitt's criticism was totally unjustified, Robinson believed. He had always played with the attitude that every ball hit in the park should be caught, and he was one of the fiercest baserunners in the game.

There were some who said DeWitt's accusations lit the fire under Robinson that inspired him to lead the Reds to the pennant and earn the Most Valuable Player Award in 1961. But Robinson said it was not anger at DeWitt that fired him up; it was the anger he directed at himself while sitting in a jail cell.

Robinson had another reason to be angry, as the racism he had encountered in the Sally League continued to plague him. After the Reds clinched the 1961 pennant in Chicago, they flew home to a noisy public celebration in the streets. Later, there was a private party for the players at a local club. But when Robinson and his teammate Vada Pinson arrived there, they were stopped at the door and

Robinson took a pay cut when he signed his 1964 contract with Reds' president Bill DeWitt (left). Assistant general manager Phil Seghi looks on. DeWitt traded Robinson in December 1965 in what was arguably the worst trade the Reds ever made.

told, "No Negroes allowed." Only after someone reminded the owner who the two men were, did he say, "Oh, you guys are all right, go right in." Pinson and Robinson walked in, went straight through the place and out the back door, and then had their own private celebration. Although they wanted to be with the rest of the team, they could not bring themselves to stay where other blacks were not wanted.

That same year, Robinson and his new bride, Barbara, tried to buy a house in Cincinnati and were shown homes only in black neighborhoods. Even the wives of the white players would not have anything to do with Barbara Robinson. Frank Robinson may have been the team leader, but off the field he was treated like a second-class citizen.

The barrier was broken just a little in 1963, when a cocky kid named Pete Rose made the team. Rose was not popular with the other players, but Pinson and Robinson felt sorry for him. When they asked Rose to join them for dinner, he jumped at the chance. The three became friends and went everywhere together.

Although he was still shy with strangers, Robinson was always available to any player who had a question or sought his advice. By his seventh season, 1962, he had become one of the team's veterans and an obvious leader. He did not hesitate to talk to a player he thought was giving less than full effort or to chew out a man for making a mental mistake.

Robinson's actions spoke even louder than his words and not even his harshest critics could complain about his performance in 1962. He played in every game despite a string of injuries that included a wrenched back, a broken toe, and a bruised right hand. He wound up with a .342 average, his best ever, along with a league-leading 51 doubles, 39 homers, and 134 RBIs. The Reds just missed as N.L. champions, finishing 3½ games behind the Giants.

Nevertheless, the pain of playing hurt most of the year and the prospect of further financial battles with the front office prompted Robinson to announce near the end of the season that he was quitting baseball at the age of 27. Nobody took the news seriously at the time—it was not the first time he had threatened to leave the game. His teammates

There were six Reds on the 1965 National League All-Star team, twice as many players as any other team represented. The players are shown here with their manager (left to right): Leo Cardenas, John Edwards, Robinson, manager Dick Sisler, Jim Maloney, Sammy Ellis, and Pete Rose.

were glad when he quickly reconsidered, but his opponents certainly were not.

Frank Robinson would never win a popularity contest among ball players. In fact, he had just lost one earlier in 1962. That year, the players elected the All-Star teams. (Today the fans do the voting.) Although he was then well on his way to a super season, Robinson was ignored in the voting.

One obvious reason for his unpopularity was his flashing spikes on the base paths. But there was more to it than that. Robinson held the old-fashioned notion that the opponent was the enemy. Most players greet each other on the field before a game, swapping small talk, asking about each other's families. Not Robinson. And when a batter reached first base, that player often has a word or two with the first baseman before the next pitch. But not with Robinson.

"Nobody who ever played this game has been more a professional," wrote Jerry Izenberg in *Sport* magazine. "Nobody who has ever played this game has been less a company man. Nobody. . . has had greater respect from his teammates and incurred greater hatred from his opponents."

Many players would have been hurt by that observation. But not Robinson. "I don't believe in that stuff on the field, being friendly," he explained. "They put you out there to win, not to socialize."

Robinson considered his lack of popularity proof that he was playing to win—and succeeding. With his teammates, he was friendly and occasionally funny. They did not really know him well, but they appreciated him as a cheerleader who shouted encouragement to them when they were at bat and said the words that picked them up on a long hot afternoon.

"He runs into walls, he stands in to pitches, he

Good friend and former teammate Pete Rose greets Robinson during the 1966 spring training season.

runs bases like a maniac," said Reds third baseman Gene Freese. "When it comes to guts, I've never seen anybody to equal him."

In the years that followed, Frank Robinson continued to lead the league in being hit by pitches, and he continued to pay the pitchers back by hitting home runs his next time at bat. Worn down by injuries—he played all of one year with a bad hand and had to swing practically one-handed—he had some seasons that would have been considered great for ordinary players but were subpar for him. Still, he carried the rest of the team. One day, when he and Vada Pinson were both chasing a fly ball, they collided and went down. When Robinson did not get up immediately, the players on the bench groaned, "There goes our money [for finishing in the first division]." The Reds stood on the dugout steps and held their breath until Robinson got up.

In the spring of 1964, Fred Hutchinson was stricken with cancer. He stayed with the team until

August, when he became too weak to continue. The Reds fought hard to win the pennant, but they lost out on the last day, finishing one game behind the Cardinals. Hutchinson died a month later.

Robinson was convinced he had the necessary qualities to be a leader, and he began to think about managing someday. At the time, there were no black managers in baseball, but he believed that he was at least as capable as some of the people he had played for. He hoped the time would come when the color of a man's skin would not be a factor. And to make sure he was ready for that day, he studied the game intently.

Every year, he had to fight for a raise from Bill DeWitt, who continued to put him down, belittle him, and chip away at his pride to hold down Robinson's salary. As he moved closer to the $100,000 level, DeWitt grew harsher in his criticism. Finally, he decided to get rid of Robinson.

At 4:20 on the afternoon of December 9, 1965, DeWitt's assistant, Phil Seghi, called Robinson to tell him he had been traded to the Baltimore Orioles in the American League, for two pitchers and a part-time outfielder. Robinson, who had been in Cincinnati for ten years, was stunned by the news.

But when a reporter called him a few minutes later to find out his reaction, Robinson simply said, "It's a challenge. I'll be in a strange league with a strange team. But I have faced challenges before and have overcome them. I'll overcome this one."

And so he did. The three players the Reds obtained for Robinson could not save the team from tumbling to seventh place the next year. But Frank Robinson's contribution to the Baltimore Orioles wound up making baseball history.

6

MEETING THE CHALLENGE

On May 8, 1966, Robinson hit a home run out of Baltimore's Memorial Stadium, a feat still unduplicated. He shakes hands with Luis Aparicio. Robinson hit home runs in 32 major-league parks.

Sitting on a bench in March 1966, Frank Robinson was burning up. It was not the Florida sun blazing down on the spring training field that had him hot under the collar, however. It was the words of Bill DeWitt, who had referred to Robinson as "an old thirty" upon trading him from the Reds. Robinson resented the implication that he was over the hill at age 30. His pride wounded, Robinson was determined to make DeWitt eat his words.

The Orioles had finished third in the league both in 1964 and 1965. But now they were hoping that Robinson would take them all the way to the top. Frank Robinson did not disappoint them.

He was always one of the first on the field and the last to leave. He was more than happy to work with young players and talked baseball with them long after the practice sessions ended. But anyone who made a careless mistake or showed a lack of hustle had to answer to him. Robinson and All-Star third baseman Brooks Robinson wasted no time in letting the rest of the league know what was in store for them. On opening day in Boston, Frank was hit by a pitch his first time at bat. Brooks followed with a home run. Then Frank added a single and a home run of his own; Brooks had three hits and a stolen base, and made some of his usual spectacular plays at third base. The O's went on to win in 13 innings at Fenway Park. And that was just the beginning. For six years the two Robinsons—the black Frank and the white Brooks—would dress in adjacent lockers without a single word of jealousy or animosity passing between them. Each was a star in his own right, and a fan of the other.

The two Robinsons led the Orioles to the 1966 A.L. pennant, and Frank finished tops in the league in batting (.316), home runs (49), and RBIs (122). He was the first to lead in all three categories since Mickey Mantle did it ten years earlier.

The Orioles met the Los Angeles Dodgers, Frank's arch rivals from the National League, in the World Series. In the first inning of game 1 he faced Don Drysdale, the man who had thrown more balls at him than any other pitcher. Robinson socked the first pitch for a two-run homer to lead the Orioles to victory. Baltimore pitchers shut out the Dodgers in the next three games, and the Orioles were world champions. It seemed fitting and proper that the only run scored in the last game was also a home run by Frank Robinson—off Don Drysdale.

Named the Most Valuable Player in the World Series, Frank received a new Corvette. He was also voted the MVP of the American League, which made him the first player to win that award in both leagues.

The Orioles showed their appreciation with a $100,000 contract for 1967, a figure that had been equaled by only four ball players: Mickey Mantle, Willie Mays, Ted Williams, and Sandy Koufax.

But Robinson was still not happy—and with good reason. Although the white Baltimore fans were cheering him in the ballpark, they would not let him live in their neighborhood. He could afford to buy the finest home, but they would not even allow him to rent one. It would be five years before the Robinsons could move into a house they truly liked, and still their white neighbors would have nothing to do with them. Finally, the Robinsons bought a house in Los Angeles and made their permanent home there.

Among the Orioles, there was no mixed socializing. On road trips, the whites for the most part never invited any black players to eat with them. Brooks Robinson would sometimes tell Frank what restaurant the players were going to, thus implying that he was welcome to join them. And sometimes Frank did. For their part, the black players did not invite the whites to their homes.

Frank Robinson and his wife, Barbara, sit in the car presented by Sport *magazine, which named Frank the outstanding player in the 1966 World Series.*

In 1968, Frank Robinson got his first chance to manage when he guided the Santurce club in the Puerto Rico winter league. He shakes hands with Santurce owner Hiram Cuevas, as Earl Weaver (standing, left) and Harry Dalton look on.

Frank may have set an example with his play on the field and as a leader in the clubhouse, but outside the ballpark he was still a loner.

The 1967 and 1968 seasons were disappointing for the Orioles. They did not come close to winning a pennant in either year. Although he was still one of the league's top hitters, Frank Robinson was seriously hobbled by injuries and illness. In June 1967, he slid into second base to break up a double play. The second baseman flipped up into the air—and came down with his knee on Robinson's head. The blow left Robinson with blurred vision and severe headaches for more than a year.

In 1968, Robinson came down with the mumps, a common childhood disease that can be quite serious when adults get it. That same season, the Orioles named Earl Weaver as their new manager. Weaver had been spending his winters managing a team in the Puerto Rican league, where Frank had played in 1954. Because Weaver could not manage two teams at a time, Robinson asked Weaver to put in a word for him with the owner of the Puerto Rican club. As a result, Frank Robinson became the first black manager in the winter league.

Now he faced a new test: to see if white players would play for a black manager. That question was quickly answered. Whatever problems he had as a manager—and he had some—color was not one of them.

Robinson did encounter one problem though, and it was one that many superstars face when they become managers: expecting other players to be capable of doing what they had done. Ty Cobb and Rogers Hornsby were two stars who never overcame this problem as managers; Frank Robinson was one who did. He learned quickly that few players had his outstanding talents. He did get upset, however, when they did not give a 100 percent effort. He also got upset with umpires, and his fiery temper got him thrown out of many games.

Although he still had a lot to learn, Robinson finished his first winter season confident that he had what it took to be a big-league manager. Now all he had to do was convince someone to give a black man a chance.

THE FIRST BLACK MANAGER

Back in Baltimore for the 1969 season, Frank Robinson was feeling fit and confident. He joined Brooks, Boog Powell, Mark Belanger, and a solid pitching staff for a three-year reign in which the Orioles totally dominated the American League. They ran away with the pennant every year, but the only World Series they won was in 1970. That victory was especially sweet for Robinson because it was over the team that had considered him "washed up" five years earlier—the Cincinnati Reds.

On June 26, 1970, Frank hit two grand-slam home runs in two innings, something only two other players have ever done. On September 13, 1971, he hit the 500th home run of his career. (When he hit number 586, his last, in 1976, it would place him fourth in the record books, behind Hank Aaron, Babe Ruth, and Willie Mays.)

Robinson was now the senior man on the team. When younger players came to him for advice, he responded eagerly; otherwise, he left them alone.

Robinson connects as Brooks Robinson waits on deck. Frank played just six years with the Orioles, but they were in the World Series four of those years. His uniform number 20 was the first number ever to be retired by Baltimore.

He also kept the team loose by running a kangaroo court, a trial court done in fun. As the self-appointed judge, he fined players for such "offenses" as yawning on the bench during a game or wearing colorful clothes to the ballpark. To keep it light, court was held only after the Orioles won.

Chicago *Tribune* writer Jerome Holtzman called Robinson one of the two most inspirational ballplayers he had seen in twenty years (the other was Mickey Mantle). "Robby does it by example," he wrote, "but also by encouraging, goading and, sometimes, by telling his teammates that they've got to do better, they've got to give 100 percent."

Earning $135,000 in 1971, Frank Robinson was one of the highest paid players of his time. But he was 35 years old then, and the Orioles had some fine youngsters ready to move up. Robinson knew

Robinson reads the headlines announcing his trade to the Dodgers. By his side are his wife, Barbara, and his children, Nichelle, age 6, and Frank, age 9.

it was very likely he would be traded, so he asked to be sent to a team near his home in California. The Orioles honored his request, and on December 2, 1971, Frank Robinson was sent to his old rivals, the L.A. Dodgers.

The Dodgers were happy to have Robinson on their side for a change, but the aging star had a disappointing 1972 season. He suffered injuries to his knees and shoulder and played in only 103 games. The Dodgers finished third and promptly traded him to the California Angels.

Robinson's two years with the Angels were not exactly heavenly. He was used mostly as a designated hitter, and his batting average fell to .245—the lowest of his 22 years in baseball. It was rumored that manager Bobby Winkles was about to be fired, and Robinson's name was mentioned as a possible replacement. But when Winkles was fired, the Angels went with the experienced Dick Williams.

Meanwhile, Robinson continued to manage in Puerto Rico each winter, winning pennants and demonstrating that he deserved a chance to manage in the the big leagues. Every time there was an opening, his name was thrown in the rumor mill. But someone else, someone white, always got the job. Robinson began to doubt that his day would ever come.

"I'm getting tired of the delays and excuses," he said. "You keep hearing about how a Maury Wills or an Elston Howard [both black] is being considered for a managerial job. They have the qualifications, but in the end someone will say they don't have the experience."

Robinson found it hard to believe that his five years of managing in Puerto Rico did not count as experience. Told that he would have to manage in the major or minor leagues to be considered, he could not help wondering how it was that so many white managers were given a chance without such experience.

Near the end of the 1974 season, the Angels released Robinson. He was picked up by the Cleveland Indians, who were suffering through a losing season and clearly needed all the help they could get. Yet on Robinson's first day in a Cleveland uniform, he was greeted on the field by a banner reading "Sickle cell anemia—the great white hope." Sickle cell anemia is a deadly disease that affects primarily black people. Though Robinson knew the message was aimed at him, he refused to let it get him down. In his younger days, such blatant racism would have made him burn with anger, but he had long since learned to deal with it.

"You can feel all kinds of anger inside you, but you have to think about what kind of person would do something like that," he said at the time. "It had to be a very sick person, and I kept telling myself that."

As soon as Robinson joined the Indians, the newspapers began predicting that the manager would be fired and replaced by Robinson. And this time, the rumors proved to be true. At the end of the season, the Indians made Frank Robinson baseball's first black manager. As he calmly faced a room filled with reporters and television cameras on October 3, 1974, Robinson expressed the hope that it would not be long before he was simply known as a manager and not always referred to as a "black manager."

Frank also acknowledged his gratitude to Jackie Robinson, who had died two years earlier. Having experienced a great deal of racial prejudice in the minor leagues and as recently as his

first day in Cleveland, Frank could well understand how hard it must have been in 1947 for the first and only black player in the majors.

"If I had one wish I was sure would be granted, it would be that Jackie Robinson could be here, seated alongside me, today," he said. He then invited Jackie's widow, Rachel Robinson, to throw out the first ball at the Indians' opening game in 1975.

Frank Robinson remained active as a player while he managed the Indians, and he could not have gotten off to a better start: In his first time at bat on opening day, he hit a home run. Unfortunately, that turned out to be one of very few happy days for him in Cleveland. Along with the glory and prestige of being a big-league manager, Robinson quickly learned that there were plenty of headaches. A player has to worry about himself and nobody else, but a manager has to deal with the problems, complaints, moods, and mistakes of twenty-five different personalities.

Baseball commissioner Bowie Kuhn offers congratulations to Robinson after he was named player-manager of the Cleveland Indians in 1975.

Shortly after he came to Cleveland, Robinson had had a run-in with star pitcher Gaylord Perry. Perry had announced that he wanted to be paid one dollar more than Robinson in 1975, a comment that left Robinson sorely offended, and created tension between them. But Perry was not his only problem. Robinson was finding it difficult to motivate the whole team to play better. He had never needed anyone to push him to play harder, and he could not understand why a professional ballplayer could not light his own fire.

The Indians struggled through the season, losing more than they won. They missed signs and failed to make simple plays. Fly balls were dropped between outfielders. The batting was weak, and the pitching was worse. Frustrated by the team's poor record, Robinson argued long and loud with the umpires and was ejected from more than one game.

Robinson had assumed that the hardest part of his job would be dealing with the newspaper, radio, and television reporters, but he soon learned that those duties were the easiest part. "The toughest part," he explained, "is coping with problems involving players, injuries, personal matters, gripes…always something."

He tried to be patient and was criticized for being too lenient. He did not require the players to be in bed at any particular time on the road, and when they abused this freedom he had to slap a curfew on them.

As a manager, he also had to deal with those players who did not get upset when the team lost as long as they got their hits. It was an attitude that, ironically, he had been accused of when he was young. Moreover, there was no enthusiasm or togetherness on the field, and it seemed clear that nobody was having fun playing the game.

A few times during the season, Robinson thought about quitting, just as he had done back in the Sally League. But he had not quit then, and he would not quit now. Instead, he called a team meeting in August and lectured the players about their lack of hustle on the field. Robinson's pep talk paid off, as the Indians went on to win 18 games and lose only 5 in September. Although they wound up fourth in their division, the strong finish gave Robinson some real hope for the next year.

Having learned from experience, Robinson was tougher from the start in 1976. But there was just so much he could do. Robinson simply did not have enough good players to do much better. The Indians again finished fourth.

Robinson's intense desire to win never wavered, however. Trailing 4-3 in the 13th inning one night in June, he did not hesitate to put himself in as a pinch-hitter. And he came through with a two-run homer to win the game. On July 6, he hit his last home run, in Baltimore, the scene of his greatest success as a player. In a game against Baltimore, Orioles catcher Elrod Hendricks slammed his helmet down when he was called out on a close play. Hendricks had been Frank's teammate at Baltimore and played for him six years in Puerto Rico. But that did not stop Robinson from arguing that Hendricks should be ejected from the game, which meant a $100 fine.

Hendricks said afterwards, "Once the game starts he gets mad at even his best friends. The whole game he was screaming at me, trying to get me mad." But Hendricks did not seem mad. "I learned from him not to let that kind of riding affect me," he explained.

8

BACK TO BALTIMORE

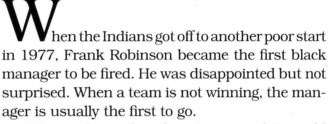

When the Indians got off to another poor start in 1977, Frank Robinson became the first black manager to be fired. He was disappointed but not surprised. When a team is not winning, the manager is usually the first to go.

"It's much tougher than I imagined it would be," he said about managing. "I learned something every day.... I learned right out that you cannot satisfy every ballplayer. I thought I could keep twenty-five players reasonably happy, but there are some people, no matter what you do, you can't make happy."

Many people—Frank Robinson included—felt he had not been given a fair chance in Cleveland; that his players simply had not had enough talent to win. And Robinson still believed he could manage a winning team. So instead of staying home with his family that winter, he went down to Mexico to manage.

Robinson returned to the big leagues in 1978 as a coach for the Orioles. Early in the season, he was asked to manage their farm team at Rochester,

As manager of the San Francisco Giants, Frank often sparred with umpires.

New York. That same season, Larry Doby became baseball's second black manager when he was hired by the Chicago White Sox.

While Robinson went back to coaching the Orioles for the next two years, a third black, Maury Wills, was named manager of the Seattle Mariners. And by the time Robinson received an offer to manage the San Francisco Giants in 1981, he was able to realize another of his goals: he was now referred to as Frank Robinson, manager, not Frank Robinson, black manager.

By then, Robinson had learned to handle players better and to give them a pat on the back when it was needed. Still, his candor in the heat of anger sometimes got him into hot water, and he sometimes wondered aloud if the umpires had it in for him and his team.

Despite such difficulties, Robinson quickly proved himself a winning manager by taking a so-so Giants team down the wire in a tight pennant race in 1982. For his work, Robinson was named National League Manager of the Year. That same year, he was elected to the Hall of Fame along with Hank Aaron. At the induction ceremony he said, "I would be remiss if I didn't tell Mrs. Jackie Robinson, sitting here, how much I appreciate everything her husband did. I know I could never have put up with the things he had to put up with."

The next two years, the Giants went downhill. When the team finished last in 1984, Robinson was fired again. This time, he took it angrily, blaming the general manager and his third-base coach (who replaced Robinson as manager) for working against him. Robinson said his biggest mistake had been changing his approach from being a demanding taskmaster to being patient and tolerant with poor performances.

When he asked what he would have done differently, he said, "I would have been myself. I would not have accepted poor play, mistakes, excuses."

Robinson returned to Baltimore as a coach in 1985 and then moved into the front office as assistant to the Orioles' president. Meanwhile, many changes of managers occurred in baseball, but no more blacks were hired.

After skidding to sixth place in 1987, the Orioles started the 1988 season by losing their first six games. They then asked Robinson to return to the dugout as manager. But things did not improve much with him at the helm. The Orioles went on to lose their first 21 games, the worst start any team ever had. They lost a grand total of 107 games that year and won only 54.

But the team made trades to bring some younger players on to the roster. And as the 1989 season began, Robinson showed that he had learned his lessons well. More experienced at blending patience with a demand for high standards and all-out play, he led baseball's youngest team into first place and kept them there for most of the season. The Orioles made it to the last series of the season, in Toronto, before the Blue Jays inched past them for the Eastern Division title. It was one of the greatest turnarounds any team had ever accomplished, and it brought Robinson his second Manager of the Year Award.

Frank Robinson still has one goal remaining: to manage a team in the World Series.

"It would be a bigger thrill," he says, "than playing in one."

He probably would not even mind if the newspapers referred to him as Frank Robinson, "first black manager to win the World Series."

CHRONOLOGY

Aug. 31, 1935	Born in Beaumont, Texas
1953	Signs with Cincinnati Reds
Apr. 28, 1956	Hits first major-league home run
1956	Named National League Rookie of the Year
Feb. 8, 1961	Arrested for carrying concealed weapon
Oct. 28, 1961	Marries Barbara Ann Cole
1961	Named National League MVP
Sept. 9, 1962	Frank Kevin Robinson is born
Aug. 8, 1965	Nichelle Robinson is born
Dec. 9, 1965	Traded to Baltimore Orioles for Milt Pappas, Jack Baldschun, and Dick Simpson
1966	Wins American League Triple Crown
1966	Wins A.L. MVP Award, first player to win MVP award in both leagues
1966	Wins World Series MVP Award
1967	Signs $100,000 contract with Orioles
1968	Becomes manager of Santurce in Puerto Rico winter league
Dec. 2, 1971	Traded to Los Angeles Dodgers
Nov. 28, 1972	Traded to California Angels
Sept. 12, 1974	Waived to Cleveland Indians
Oct. 3, 1974	Named manager of Cleveland Indians
July 6, 1976	Hits his 586th—and last—home run
June 19, 1977	Fired as Indians manager
1981	Hired as manager of San Francisco Giants
1982	Elected to Hall of Fame; named N.L. Manager of the Year
1984	Fired as manager of San Francisco Giants
1988	Hired to manage Baltimore Orioles
1989	Wins second Manager of the Year Award

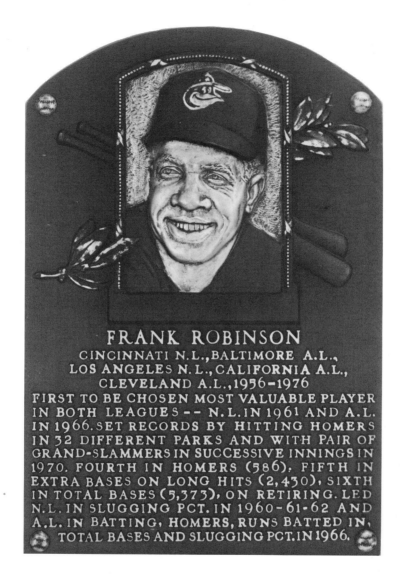

FRANK ROBINSON

CINCINNATI N.L., BALTIMORE A.L.,
LOS ANGELES N.L., CALIFORNIA A.L.,
CLEVELAND A.L., 1956-1976
FIRST TO BE CHOSEN MOST VALUABLE PLAYER
IN BOTH LEAGUES -- N.L. IN 1961 AND A.L.
IN 1966. SET RECORDS BY HITTING HOMERS
IN 32 DIFFERENT PARKS AND WITH PAIR OF
GRAND-SLAMMERS IN SUCCESSIVE INNINGS IN
1970. FOURTH IN HOMERS (586), FIFTH IN
EXTRA BASES ON LONG HITS (2,430), SIXTH
IN TOTAL BASES (5,373), ON RETIRING. LED
N.L. IN SLUGGING PCT. IN 1960-61-62 AND
A.L. IN BATTING, HOMERS, RUNS BATTED IN,
TOTAL BASES AND SLUGGING PCT. IN 1966.

MAJOR LEAGUE STATISTICS

CINCINNATI REDS, BALTIMORE ORIOLES, LOS ANGELES DODGERS, CALIFORNIA ANGELS, CLEVELAND INDIANS

YEAR	TEAM	G	AB	R	H	2B	3B	HR	RBI	BA	SB
1956	CIN N	152	572	122	166	27	6	38	83	.290	8
1957		150	611	97	197	29	5	29	75	.322	10
1958		148	554	90	149	25	6	31	83	.269	10
1959		146	540	106	168	31	4	36	125	.311	18
1960		139	464	86	138	33	6	31	83	.297	13
1961		153	545	117	176	32	7	37	124	.323	22
1962		162	609	134	208	51	2	39	136	.342	18
1963		140	482	79	125	19	3	21	91	.259	26
1964		156	568	103	174	38	6	29	96	.306	23
1965		156	582	109	172	33	5	33	113	.296	13
1966	BAL A	155	576	122	182	34	2	49	122	.316	8
1967		129	479	83	149	23	7	30	94	.311	2
1968		130	421	69	113	27	1	15	52	.268	11
1969		148	539	111	166	19	5	32	100	.308	9
1970		132	471	88	144	24	1	25	78	.306	2
1971		133	455	82	128	16	2	28	99	.281	3
1972	LA N	103	342	41	86	6	1	19	59	.251	2
1973	CAL A	147	534	85	142	29	0	30	97	.266	1
1974	2 teams	CAL A (129G – .251)			CLE A (15G – .200)						
	total	144	477	81	117	27	3	22	68	.245	5
1975		49	118	19	28	5	0	9	24	.237	0
1976		36	67	5	15	0	0	3	10	.224	0
Totals		2808	10006	1829	2943	528	72	586	1812	.294	204
League Championship Series (3 years)		9	34	6	7	3	0	2	5	.206	0
World Series (5 years)		26	92	19	23	2	1	8	14	.250	0
All-Star games **Total**		11	24	2	6	0	0	1	1	.250	1

FURTHER READING

Brosnan, Jim. *Great Rookies of the Major Leagues*. New York: Random House, 1966.

Daley, Arthur. *All the Home Run Kings*. New York: G. P. Putnam, 1972.

Hirshberg, Al. *Frank Robinson, Born Leader*. New York: G.P. Putnam, 1973.

Liss, Howard. *Triple-Crown Winners*. New York: Julian Messner, 1969.

Robinson, Frank, and Al Silverman. *My Life In Baseball*. New York: Doubleday & Co., 1968.

Robinson, Frank, and Berry Stainback. *Extra Innings*. New York: McGraw-Hill, 1988.

Robinson, Frank, and Dave Anderson. *Frank: The First Year*. New York: Holt, Rinehart & Winston, 1976.

Schneider, Russell J. *Frank Robinson, The Making of a Manager*. New York: Coward, McCann & Geoghegan, 1976.

INDEX

PICTURE CREDITS

AP/Wide World Photos: pp. 2, 11, 18, 20, 24, 29, 32, 35, 36, 38, 40, 43, 44, 48, 51, 54, 58; National Baseball Library, Cooperstown, NY: pp. 22, 26, 46, 60; Oakland Public Library, Oakland, CA: p. 14; UPI/Bettmann Newsphotos: p. 8

NORMAN MACHT was a minor league general manager with the Milwaukee Braves and Baltimore Orioles organizations and has been a stock broker and college professor. His work has appeared in *The BallPlayers*, *The Sporting News*, *Baseball Digest* and *Sports Heritage*, and he is the co-author with Dick Bartell of *Rowdy Richard*. Norman Macht lives in Newark, Delaware.

JIM MURRAY, veteran sports columnist of the *Los Angeles Times*, is one of America's most acclaimed writers. He has been named "America's Best Sportswriter" by the National Association of Sportscasters and Sportswriters 14 times, was awarded the Red Smith Award, and was twice winner of the National Headliner Award. In addition, he was awarded the J. G. Taylor Spink Award in 1987 for "meritorious contributions to baseball writing." With this award came his 1988 induction into the National Baseball Hall of Fame in Cooperstown, New York. In 1990, Jim Murray was awarded the Pulitzer Prize for Commentary.

EARL WEAVER is the winningest manager in Baltimore Orioles history by a wide margin. He compiled 1,480 victories in his 17 years at the helm. After managing eight different minor league teams, he was given the chance to lead the Orioles in 1968. Under his leadership the Orioles finished lower than second place in the American League East only four times in 17 years. One of only 12 managers in big league history to have managed in four or more World Series, Earl was named Manager of the Year in 1979. The popular Weaver had his number 5 retired in 1982, joining Brooks Robinson, Frank Robinson, and Jim Palmer, whose numbers were retired previously. Earl Weaver continues his association with the professional baseball scene by writing, broadcasting, and coaching.